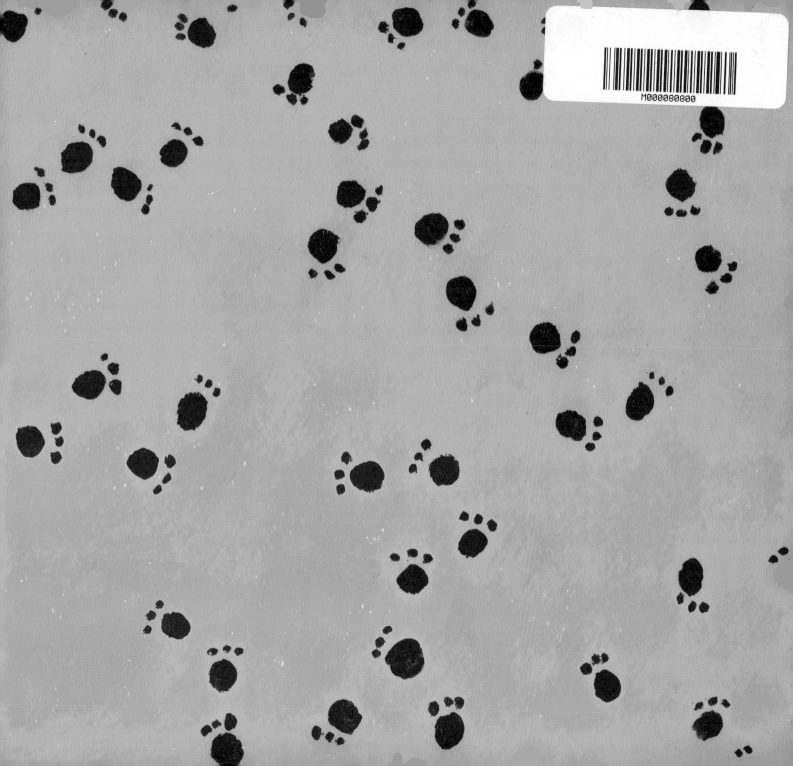

M000080800

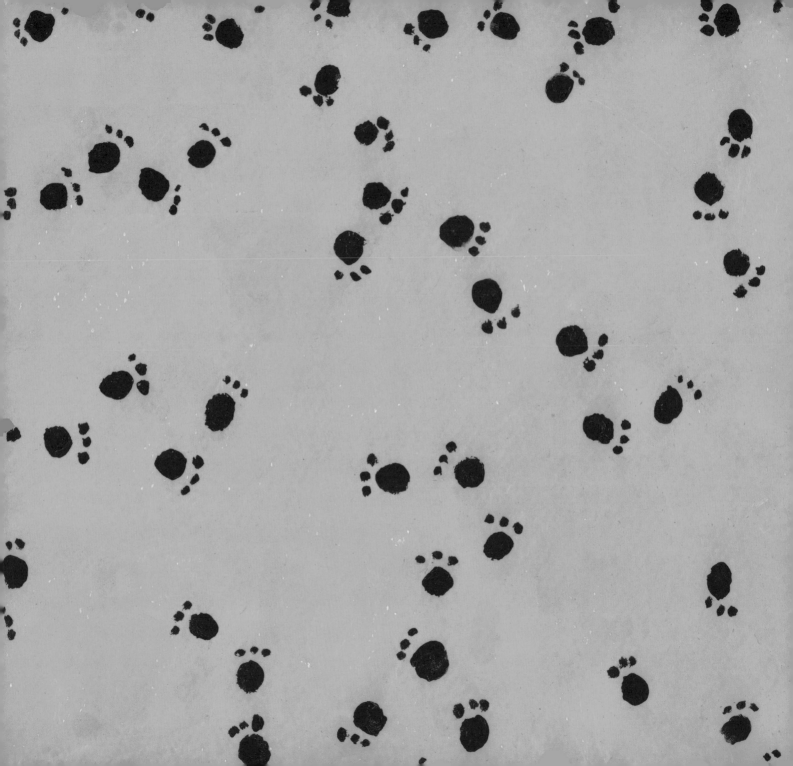

nancy drosd
&
danielle weil

40 most wanted cats

SMITHMARK

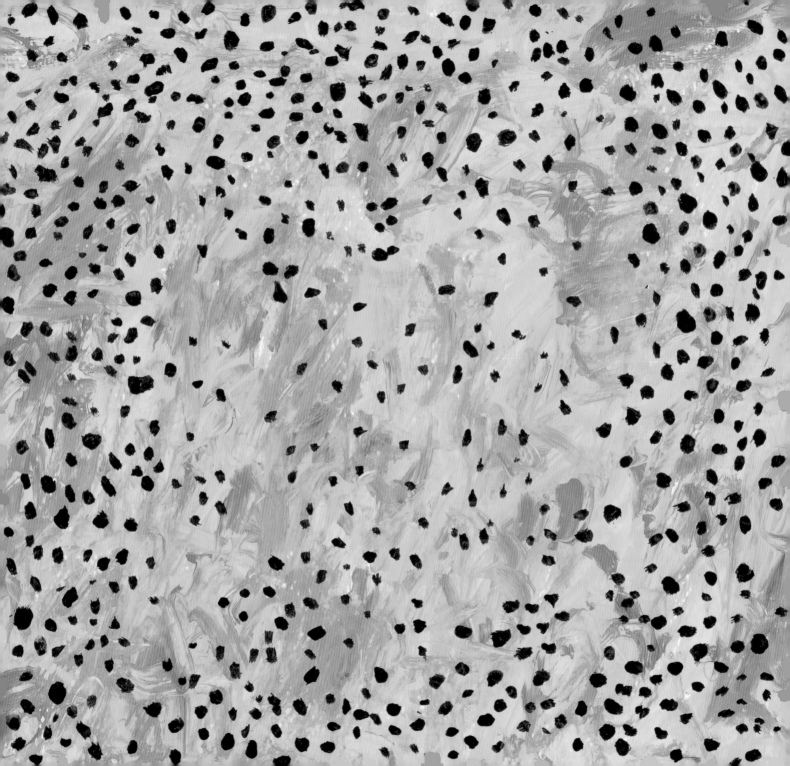

everything that
deceives may be
said to enchant

Plato

Copyright © 1998
Nancy Drosd and Danielle Weil

All rights reserved. No part of this
publication may be reproduced, stored
in a retrieval system or transmitted
in any form by any means electronic,
mechanical, photocopying or otherwise
without first obtaining written
permission of the copyright owner.

This edition published in 1998 by
SMITHMARK Publishers, a division
of U.S. Media Holdings, Inc.,
115 West 18th Street, New York, NY 10011.

SMITHMARK books are available for
bulk purchase for sales promotion
and premium use. For details write
or call the manager of special sales,
SMITHMARK Publishers,
115 West 18th Street, New York, NY 10011;
212-519-1300.

ISBN: 0-7651-9062-1

Printed in Hong Kong

10 9 8 7 6 5 4 3 2 1

Library of Congress
Catalog Card Number: 97-62151

Quote: Plato, *The Republic*

Editorial Director:
        Elizabeth Viscott Sullivan
Editor: Tricia Levi
Designer: Karen Engelmann

wanted for...

failure to
respond
to a
summons

cultivation of a controlled substance

making & crank calls

aggravated assault

5
evading arrest

intent to commit mayhem

speeding

passing
bad checks

disturbing the peace

9

mis-
appropriation
of funds

fishing without a license

possession of stolen goods

malice afore-
thought

loitering

harboring
a fugitive

fleeing the scene of an accident

indecent exposure

18 art forgery

unlawful
assembly

hijacking

voyeurism

eavesdropping

product
tampering

25
shoplifting

criminal solicitation

27

gambling

littering

stalking

un-
authorized
use of a
vehicle

drinking
under the
age limit

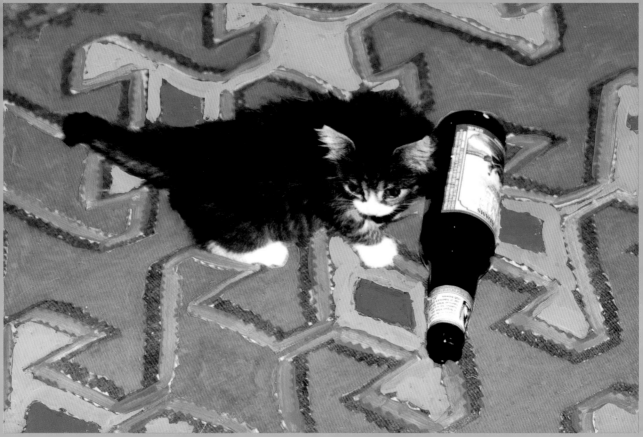

menacing

catnapping

industrial espionage

vagrancy

tampering
with
evidence

forced
entry

embezzling

conspiracy

acknowledgments

michael agrofolio

kathryn & robert altman

jan ameen

catherine audette

joanne barkan

coco brown

robert brown

florence & rudolph drosd

judy drosd

beth dunlop

karen engelmann

kendall hammersly

eric & ann hanson

jeri jenkins

kiki

nancy kramer

michael lax

tricia levi

cindy & david major

nancy mannucci

amy & roger mennell

dr. alexander jon miller, dvm

mingus

gerald moore

lisa newlin

virginia reed

chauncey wolf rothchild

susan & john rothchild

(& noodle, strudel,
snuffy, fluffy
and picky)

jeffrey & alice schwartz

sue shapiro

ina backman shoenberg

joey skaags

leslie stoker